Developing
Grade 4 Reading Fluency

Written by
Trisha Callella

Avicota

Editor: Teri L. Applebaum
Illustrator: Ann Iosa
Cover Illustrator: Chris Ellithorpe
Designer: Mary Gagné
Cover Designer: Mary Gagné
Art Director: Tom Cochrane
Project Director: Carolea Williams

Table of Contents

Introduction

Learning to read is a systematic, learned process. Once students can read individual words, they need to learn to put those words together to form sentences. Then, students must learn to read those sentences fluently to comprehend not only the meaning of each word but also the meaning of an entire sentence. Students' reading fluency develops as they learn to break sentences into phrases and to "chunk" words together into phrases as they read. As students read sentences in phrases, they develop better comprehension of each sentence's meaning.

Use the lessons in *Developing Reading Fluency* to meet district, state, and national reading standards as you teach students how to develop reading fluency. The first four sections are arranged sequentially to help you implement fluency modeling, fluency practice by students, and then students' application of fluency strategies. Use the activities to help students build upon the skills they learned in the previous section. The final two sections of the book contain additional instruction to provide intervention for students having difficulties. The book features the following strategies to improve students' reading fluency:

- **Interactive Read-Alouds:** Use modeled and choral reading with the whole class or small groups to increase students' listening comprehension and to give them experience with rereading short rhymed phrases.
- **Read-Arounds:** Help students learn high-frequency and content words and practice reading text in phrases as they work in small groups.
- **Plays for Two:** Use these simple scripts to have students practice with a partner repeated oral reading strategies as they develop phrasing and fluency.
- **Reader's Theater:** Have students work in groups of four to practice rereading a script until they can fluently read their part in front of an audience. Use the performances as a culminating activity to have students apply all the reading strategies they have learned.
- **Phrasing Memory Challenges:** Invite students who are still not reading with phrasing and fluency to use their auditory memory to repeat phrases as you or a peer tutor models correct reading.
- **Intervention Instruction:** Use these activities with individuals or small groups to intervene with students who still struggle with reading fluency. These activities enable students to identify and practice expression, intonation, and the natural flow of fluency.

The activities in this book provide students with a variety of reading experiences. The themes and genres included in each section will motivate students to not only read the text but to read with expression, intonation, and a natural flow. Students will build enthusiasm and confidence as they begin to increase their comprehension and as they successfully apply reading strategies to their everyday reading!

Fluency

Reading fluency is the ability to read with expression, intonation, and a natural flow that sounds like talking. Fluency is not the speed at which one reads. That is the reading rate. A fluent reader does read quickly; however, he or she also focuses on phrased units of meaning. A student may read quickly but may not necessarily be fluent. Students who read too quickly often skip over punctuation. This inhibits comprehension because punctuation helps convey the meaning. Fluent readers have developed automaticity. This means that they have a solid bank of sight words on which they can rely and that are automatic. Fluent readers can then focus their reading on understanding the message rather than decoding the text. Reading is decoding with comprehension. Fluent readers do both. They read without thinking about how they are reading, and they understand what they are reading.

What does a student who lacks fluency sound like?
A student who lacks fluency may sound choppy, robotic, or speedy.

How does repeated oral reading increase fluency?
Research shows that students increase their fluency when they read and reread the same passage aloud several times. The support that teachers give students during oral reading by modeling the text and providing guidance and feedback enhances their fluency development. Using this strategy, students gradually become better readers and their word recognition, speed, accuracy, and fluency all increase as a result. Their comprehension also improves because they are bridging the gap between reading for word recognition and reading for meaning.

Should I worry about fluency with students who are emergent readers?
Bad habits can be hard to break. Research has found that poor reading habits stand in the way of students becoming fluent readers. Research has also found that students can and do become fluent even as emergent readers. Those emergent, fluent readers carry that fluency onto more difficult text and therefore have a higher level of comprehension. Fluency activities should be incorporated into every classroom, beginning in kindergarten with modeled reading, shared reading, guided reading, and independent reading.

How do fluency and phrasing work together?
Phrasing is the link between decoding the meaning of the text and reading the text fluently. Phrasing is the way that a reader groups the words. A lack of phrasing results in staccato reading, "word calling," and decoding. A fluent reader reads quickly in phrased chunks that are meaningful. Read the information on page 5 to learn more about phrasing.

Phrasing

A student who reads in phrases reads words in meaningful groups. Phrasing helps a student understand that the text carries meaning. A phrase is a group of words that the reader says together and reads together. The way the words are grouped affects the meaning. This is why phrasing affects reading comprehension.

What does phrasing sound like?

Consider how the same sentence can have different meanings depending on the way the words are grouped, or phrased. It clearly affects the comprehension of what is read. For example:

> Patti Lee is my best friend.
> Patti, Lee is my best friend.

Who is the best friend? It depends on how the sentence is read. In this example, punctuation also affects phrasing.

What causes incorrect phrasing?

A student may read with incorrect phrasing for a number of reasons. First of all, many students rely too much on phonics. This leads to a dependency on decoding. When students focus on decoding, they neglect the message. They turn into expert "word callers." Incorrect phrasing can also result from a lack of attention to punctuation. Some students ignore punctuation altogether, which will result in incorrect phrasing, will affect their fluency, and will hurt their comprehension.

What can I do to teach and improve phrasing?

1. Use the activities in this book. They are all researched, teacher-tested, and student-approved, and they will help students experience reading fluency success.

2. Stop pointing to each word during shared reading because that reinforces word-by-word reading. Once students can point and read with one-to-one correspondence, begin shared reading with a finger sweep under phrases. (Finger sweeps look like a stretched out "u.") This strategy models and reinforces phrasing.

3. Read and reread.

4. Model. Model. Model.

5. Echo read.

6. Make flash cards of common phrases to help students train their eyes to see words in groups rather than as individual words.

7. Tape-record students as they read. Let them listen to improvements they make in phrasing and intonation.

How to Use This Book

The activities in this book provide fun and easy strategies that will help students develop reading fluency. Getting started is simple.

- Use the Stages of Fluency Development chart on page 7 to assess students' ability. Take notes as students read aloud, and then refer to the chart to see at what stage of fluency development they are. Use this information to create a plan of action and to decide on which skills the whole class, groups of students, and individuals need to focus.
- Use the Fantastic Five Format on page 8 with the whole class, small groups, or individuals. This format provides a guideline for developing reading fluency that will work with any genre. Copy the reproducible, and use it as a "cheat sheet" when you give guided instruction. You will find the format effective in helping you with modeling, teaching, guiding, and transferring phrased and fluent reading to independent reading.
- Refer to the Teacher Tips on page 9 before you begin using the activities in this book. These tips include helpful information that will assist you as you teach all the students in your classroom to read fluently and, as a result, improve their comprehension of text.

Fluency Activities and Strategies

The first four sections of this book have been sequentially arranged for you to first model fluency, then have students practice fluency, and finally have them independently apply their newly learned skills. Each section has an introductory page to help you get started. It includes

- an explanation of how the activities in that section relate to fluency development
- the strategies students will use to complete the activities
- a materials list
- step-by-step directions for preparing and presenting the activities
- an idea for how to extend the activities

Each section opener is followed by a set of fun reproducible reading materials that are designed to excite and motivate students about developing reading fluency. Within each section, the readability of the reproducibles increases in difficulty to provide appropriate reading material for fourth graders who read at different levels.

Intervention Activities and Strategies

The last two sections of the book provide additional instruction and practice to help students who have difficulty with reading fluency. The Phrasing Memory Challenges section contains several readings designed to be used one-on-one between a teacher or peer and a struggling student. The Intervention Instruction section contains several activities designed for use with individuals or small groups. Each activity has its own page of directions that lists strategies, an objective, materials, and step-by-step directions. Reassess students often to determine their reading fluency level and their need for intervention.

Stages of Fluency Development

Stage	What You Observe	What to Teach for Fluency
1	• many miscues • too much emphasis on meaning • storytelling based on pictures • sounds fluent but not reading what is written down • playing "teacher" while reading	• print carries the meaning
2	• tries to match what he or she says with what is written on the page • one-to-one correspondence • finger pointing and "voice pointing" • staccato reading, robotic reading	• phrasing and fluency • focus on meaning • read like talking • high-frequency words • purpose of punctuation
3	• focuses on the meaning of print • may use bookmarks • focuses more on print than picture • no longer voice points • laughs, giggles, or comments while reading	• phrasing and fluency • focus on what makes sense and looks right • purpose of punctuation • proper expression and intonation
4	• reads books with more print than pictures • wants to talk about what he or she read • reads like talking with phrasing • reads punctuation with expression • laughs, giggles, or comments while reading	• shades of meaning • making connections

Fantastic Five Format

Step 1

Modeled Fluency

Model reading with fluency so that students understand the text and what they are supposed to learn.

Step 2

Echo Reading

Read one part. Have students repeat the same part.

Step 3

Choral Reading

Read together. This prepares students to take over the task of reading.

Step 4

Independent Fluency

Have students read to you.

Step 5

Reverse Echo Reading

Have students read to you, and then repeat their phrasing, expression, and fluency. Students have now taken over the task of reading.

Developing Reading Fluency • Gr. 4 © 2003 Creative Teaching Press

Teacher Tips

1. Be aware of how you arrange rhymes, stories, and poems in a pocket chart. Often, teachers put each line in a separate pocket. When teachers do this, students do not recognize phrases and they begin to think that sentences always end on the right. (That is one reason why students often put a period at the end of every line in their writing journals.) Instead, cut the sentences or rhymes into meaningful phrased chunks so that students see and read what you model and teach.

2. If you use guided reading in your classroom, incorporate time for students to reread familiar books. Keep guided reading books that were once used for instructional purposes in bins that are color-coded to represent different ability levels. Have each student choose a book to reread as a warm-up every time you meet. This helps students put phrasing and fluency instruction into practice. Remember, use books that are appropriate to students' independent-reading level (books that can be read with 85 percent accuracy).

3. Write a daily Morning Message that follows a predictable format. Follow the Fantastic Five Format on page 8 to develop phrasing and fluency and improve reading comprehension.

4. Have a Student of the Day tell you three things about himself or herself. Model for the class how to write the student's information in phrases on a piece of white construction paper. Read it in phrases and choral read it for fluency. Reread all of the information about previous Students of the Day prior to writing about the new Student. Bind the pages together into a class book, and have students read it independently or take it home to share with their family.

5. Once a student matches speech to print, do not allow him or her to point when reading. It is important to train students' eyes to look at words in groups rather than at one word at a time. While reading aloud, fluent readers look at many words ahead of what they read.

6. If students must use bookmarks to track words as they read, have them hold the bookmark just above the line of print they are reading rather than just under the line. When students use a bookmark under a line of print, the bookmark blocks the next line. This keeps students from reading fluently because they cannot see the ending punctuation. Try it—you will find that you cannot read fluently with a bookmark under the line you read. You will be amazed how this small change affects students' reading.

Learn to read with fluency!

Interactive Read-Alouds

Comprehension begins at the listening stage. Students understand what they hear before they understand what they read. That is why research supports reading aloud to students books and stories that are above their reading level. Reading aloud builds vocabulary, models thinking aloud, and models phrasing and fluency. This activity takes reading aloud a step further by including rhymed phrases that students will then use to apply the repeated oral reading strategy. The structure of this activity will keep students actively listening.

Strategies: repeated oral reading, modeled fluency, choral reading, active listening

Materials
• overhead projector/transparencies or chart paper (optional)

Directions

1. Choose one story, and make one copy of the reproducible. (The story "The Magic Elevator" has two pages.) Copy a class set of the corresponding rhymed phrases. Or, as an option, make an overhead transparency of the reproducible or write the rhymed phrases on the board or chart paper.

2. NOTE: Do not photocopy the story for students. This activity is designed to build students' listening comprehension. They need to hear phrasing and fluency modeled by you in order to replicate it in their own reading.

3. Give each student a copy of the rhymed phrases, or display the phrases so all the students can see them. Read aloud the phrases, and have students practice reading them. Tell students that you will read aloud a story and that they will read aloud the rhymed phrases each time you point to them. (Point to the class each time you see an asterisk in the story.)

4. For "Eating the Layers of Earth" on page 18, gather 1 bag of graham cracker crumbs, 1 cup of peanut butter, 1 round nut, and a plastic knife for each student. Invite students to perform the experiment in the story as you read aloud the story.

5. Read aloud the story. Model good phrasing, intonation, and fluency.

6. Throughout the story, stop at each asterisk, point to the students, and have them read the rhymed phrases, with increased fluency each time.

Extension

Many of the rhymed phrases lend themselves to movements. Make up silly movements that students can do as they read their part. This will maximize active listening. Try movements such as clicking tongues, clapping, stomping feet, moving hands like waves in the ocean, moving hands up together and then parting them in opposite ways, nodding heads, hopping, turning around, and cross-lateral movements.

Safety Sal

Hello boys and girls! My name is Safety Sal. I'm here to talk to you about safety. You already know the basics, since you are fourth graders. However, we will be learning about the details of safety at home, at school, and at play. I'll need your help. Whenever I point to you, you will read a little chant in unison. Let's practice first. ✳

Let's start off by discussing bicycle safety rules. If you are going to ride your bike at night, it is important to make sure that you have headlights and reflectors on your bike. This is to make sure that cars and people on the road can see you. Another good thing to have on your bike is a horn, just in case of an emergency or if someone gets in your way. You already know about how to protect your head by wearing a helmet, but you should also wear knee pads and elbow pads while on your bicycle. They will protect your bones in the case of a fall. What's our motto? ✳

Let's move on to home safety. I am sure you know all of the basics. Never open your door to strangers. Don't give out information over the telephone. Never tell anyone that your parents aren't home. Now, let's look at some of the adult safety tips that you can use at your house. There should be at least one smoke detector on each floor. The best locations are near the kitchen, in the hallway, and outside the bedroom doors. Make sure that the batteries are always charged. Keep a fire extinguisher on each floor as well. What do we always want to remember? ✳

We also want to think about school safety. In the case of a fire, your teacher is prepared to get you out safely. What you need to remember is not to panic. Just follow your teacher's instructions and you will be safe. When you ride on a school bus, you need to sit in your seat and be quiet. This will help the bus driver concentrate on driving so you will arrive safely. What do we know about safety? ✳

Finally, there is Internet safety. You can have a lot of fun on the Internet. Perhaps you like to e-mail or send instant messages to your friends and family. You might do some of your homework or research on the Internet. There are so many things that you can do! Like anything else, there are safety rules for safe use. The Internet is just like a city. Anyone can go there. You don't know the people. You need to think of the Internet as a place where many strangers could go. Therefore, you want to use your "stranger danger" safety knowledge. Never e-mail people you don't know. Ask your parents' permission before using the Internet. Don't give out any information about yourself or your family. What are you thinking right now? ✳

Excellent! Well, I can see that you already knew most of what Safety Sal came to talk to you about today. You are one clever group of students. I wish all of you a safe life at school, at home, and at play. Remember . . . ✳

Safety Sal
Rhymed Phrases

Safety first! Know the rules! That's what we say.

When you know the safety rules, it's more fun when you play!

Safety in your house. Safety at school.

Safety on the computer. It's a really great tool!

We know who it's safe to be around.

We know how to keep ourselves safe and sound!

- -

Safety Sal
Rhymed Phrases

Safety first! Know the rules! That's what we say.

When you know the safety rules, it's more fun when you play!

Safety in your house. Safety at school.

Safety on the computer. It's a really great tool!

We know who it's safe to be around.

We know how to keep ourselves safe and sound!

The Magic Elevator

"Come on, Kendra! We have to hurry! Mom and dad will be home in an hour, so we don't have much time!" "Okay, Garrett! Relax! I'm coming! I just want to make sure that the house will look good when mom and dad come home. Where do you want to go today?" asked Kendra. ✳

Last month, Kendra and Garrett moved into a new apartment building with their parents. It had an elevator to take you to any of the sixteen floors. While on the elevator three days after moving in, they discovered that it was magic! It didn't seem like anyone else in the building knew about it. They couldn't figure out why it was magic for them but not for anyone else. ✳ Their parents didn't know anything about it! They wouldn't even know themselves if they hadn't accidentally said the magic words. This is how it all started.

Kendra and Garrett were going down to the pool to meet their parents when Garrett jokingly said, "Up, up, and away!" The next thing they knew, the elevator stopped and began going up! They were supposed to be going DOWN! They waited to see what would happen next. The doors opened between two floors! They couldn't help but take a peek, since they were such curious children. They saw buffalo! They looked at each other. They looked at the buffalo. They really did see them. They didn't know what to do, so they did what any curious kids would do. They got out of the elevator to investigate. This is when they realized, ✳

They were so excited! They were in the middle of a range with buffalo roaming free. There wasn't another person around anywhere. Since they thought they would be missed, they went back into the elevator. They went downstairs and joined their parents at the pool. Meanwhile, they were both thinking to themselves, ✳

The Magic Elevator

As soon as their parents tucked them into bed and said goodnight, they began discussing what had happened. They agreed that they couldn't be crazy, since they had both seen the same thing. Being inquisitive children, they agreed to return to the elevator to try it again. Since they were also rather clever, they realized that it must have been what Garrett had said that made the elevator magical. All night long they dreamed. ✱

Every day since then, they have visited that elevator for one reason or another. Sometimes it was to get something that they had forgotten. Other times it was to do some chores. In any case, they came up with tons of excuses to return to the elevator together. Every time Garrett said, "Up, up, and away!" the elevator moved upward, stopped between floors, and a new adventure began! So far, they had been to the rain forest, the plains, an old Native American reservation, a mining town where gold had just been discovered, and the base of a volcano.

They agreed that their new apartment building was the greatest place they had ever lived. Constantly going through their minds was the thought, ✱

They considered telling their new friends on the fifth floor, but then they agreed that the more people who found out the less their chances of future travels would be. So they decided to keep it a secret. They spent much of their time at home and in school thinking, ✱

Today, they were going to try to see if there was a way to request a specific destination. Could they say the name of a town and end up there? Was there a way to pick a specific day or place? Was it possible for them to control the magic? They were walking as fast as possible when they suddenly stopped dead in their tracks! NO! It couldn't be! Please say it wasn't so! They thought, ✱ Then, they yelled, "NOOOOOO!"

What do you think happened?

Developing Reading Fluency • Gr. 4 © 2003 Creative Teaching Press

The Magic Elevator
Rhymed Phrases

It's time for the Magic Elevator ride.

There is no place that we would rather hide.

The Magic Elevator will take us somewhere,

To another time or place—if we dare.

"Up, up, and away!" is all we need to say.

Then the Magic Elevator whisks us away,

To a time in the future or a time long ago,

To any place we want to go.

Would you like to join us and come along?

Learning about another place could never be wrong!

Interactive Read-Alouds

Attitude Is Everything!

Hello boys and girls! I'm Attitude Andy. I came here today to talk to you about having a positive attitude. We all know how boring it gets to listen to other people complain. However, many of us think it's a different story when *we* complain. Well, I'm here to tell you that it isn't. Attitude is everything! When you complain, it bothers everyone who has to listen to you. Not to mention the fact that it accomplishes absolutely nothing! So, let's meet some friends and decide if they get an A for Awesome Attitude or if they need an AA for Attitude Adjustment. I'm going to introduce you to some different people. You must decide whether they have earned an A or an AA. If they earned an AA, then you will say this chant together. ✳ Here we go!

Hi, I'm Wendell. I don't like school. It's too hard. I can't do the work. I just want to stay home. Nobody would care anyway. It doesn't matter anyhow. *(Teacher: Pause and ask the class whether Wendall earned an A or an **AA**. Wait for them to say the chant.)* ✳

Hi, Wendell. My name is Mervin. I don't know what you could possibly dislike about school. It's so fun! Every day we learn new things that help us get smarter. You need to look on the bright side. If you don't like your life right now, then you need to do something about it. Go to school. Learn. Try your best. A better education is exactly what you need. Then, you can do whatever you want in your future. Learning is the best thing you can do. Just open up your mind! *(Teacher: Pause and ask the class whether Mervin earned an **A** or an AA.)*

Hello, I'm Janice. I don't know who Wendell thinks he is. Nobody wants to listen to him whine. It's not like anyone can do anything to help him like school. He is in control of his own decisions. He needs to change his whole attitude. If he expects to not like school, then he won't. If he expects to like and do well in school, then he will. I love school and I do well. He would have more friends if he would get rid of his negative attitude! *(Teacher: Pause and ask the class whether Janice earned an A or an **AA**. Wait for them to say the chant.)* ✳

Hi! I'm Alex. School is a waste of my time! I don't have any friends and everyone makes fun of me. I don't like school. I want to quit and stay home. *(Teacher: Pause and ask the class whether Alex earned an A or an **AA**. Wait for them to say the chant.)* ✳

Well now, let's think about these people we have just met. Who would you want to be friends with? Do you think that Alex's attitude has anything to do with his lack of friends? What should everyone remember? ✳

Developing Reading Fluency • Gr. 4 © 2003 Creative Teaching Press

Attitude Is Everything!
Rhymed Phrases

I won't say that I can't do it.

I won't say that I don't care.

I know it's rude and inconsiderate.

I know to others it's just not fair.

I need to stop being selfish,

Thinking the world revolves around me.

I need to grant someone else's wish.

To think positive—my attitude's the key!

- -

Attitude Is Everything!
Rhymed Phrases

I won't say that I can't do it.

I won't say that I don't care.

I know it's rude and inconsiderate.

I know to others it's just not fair.

I need to stop being selfish,

Thinking the world revolves around me.

I need to grant someone else's wish.

To think positive—my attitude's the key!

Developing Reading Fluency • Gr. 4 © 2003 Creative Teaching Press

Interactive Read-Alouds

Eating the Layers of Earth

Theme: science experiment

Let's review what we know about the planet Earth! The surface of Earth changes due to water, wind, and ice that cause weathering and erosion. When rocks are broken down into sand, soil, and other particles it is called weathering. We also know that erosion changes Earth's landforms by moving rock and soil. Now, we are going to learn more about Earth in a very fun way.

You will each receive the following materials: 1 bag of graham cracker crumbs, 1 cup of peanut butter, 1 round nut, and a plastic knife. You will be making a tasty model of Earth. Sometimes, scientists discover something but are unable to go investigate in a hands-on fashion. This is usually because it would be too dangerous. This is the case when scientists investigate the layers of Earth. Therefore, they make a smaller version of the planet and compare it to the real thing. Today, you will be scientists doing just that! Let's begin by saying our motto together. ✷

Now, what do we know about Earth's core? It is at the center of Earth and is made up mainly of iron. Therefore, out of all of the materials you have, what do you think we will use to represent the core in our model? That's right—the nut! ✷ Pick up your nut. What is the next layer going away from the core? ✷ That's right—the mantle.

What do we know about Earth's mantle? It is made up of rock and is solid. It is between the crust and the core. It is very hot and holds the magma, which we see as lava when a volcano erupts. It is much thicker than the crust. ✷ What do you think we will use to represent Earth's mantle? That's right—the peanut butter!

Roll your core in the peanut butter. As you do that, let's say our chant. ✷ Now we have the core and mantle. The outermost layer, as you know, is Earth's crust. This layer is a very thin layer of rock. What do you think we will use to represent the crust? That's right—the graham cracker crumbs. This gives us a chance to visualize the thickness and order of the layers. What are they again? ✷

Now, we are going to put these in the freezer for a short time. When they are more solid, you will cut them in half and analyze them as if you were a scientist analyzing Earth's layers. We know that would be an impossible task, so that's why scientists make models just like the one you made. ✷

Developing Reading Fluency • Gr. 4 © 2003 Creative Teaching Press

Eating the Layers of Earth
Rhymed Phrases

From the outside in, it's the crust, mantle, and core.

The layers of Earth we will know a little more.

We're making a model so that we can understand

Exactly what scientists are discovering about our land.

Eating the Layers of Earth
Rhymed Phrases

From the outside in, it's the crust, mantle, and core.

The layers of Earth we will know a little more.

We're making a model so that we can understand

Exactly what scientists are discovering about our land.

Interactive Read-Alouds

Read-Arounds

According to research, one reason why students do not read with phrasing and fluency is that they do not have a solid base of high-frequency words and sight words, which is required for reading books independently. Research recommends activities that give students practice with frequently used words. This will in turn help with phrasing and fluency because students will not need to slow down to decode as often. The Read-Around cards in this section are already written in phrases (spaces between groups of words), so students can see and better understand how to read words in groups. The Read-Around cards are designed for groups of two to four students. This allows for optimal amounts of practice and active involvement. The phrases on the cards are short and simple to help students focus directly on reading phrases and practicing high-frequency and content words.

Strategies: phrased reading; repeated oral reading; active listening; reading high-frequency, content, and sight words

Materials
- construction paper or tagboard
- scissors
- envelopes

Directions

1. Choose a set of cards (e.g., prefixes, science concepts), and copy the cards on construction paper or tagboard. (The set of cards for grammar and writing terms is three pages. The other sets are two pages.) Cut apart the cards, and laminate them so that they can be reused throughout the school year. Put the cards in an envelope, and write the title (e.g., *Prefixes*) on the envelope.

2. Give a set of cards to a small group of students so that each student has one to three cards. Review with students the pronunciation and meaning of the bold words and phrases on their clue cards so that they are familiar and comfortable with them (or preteach the words).

3. Explain that students will play a listening and reading game. Model how the game works and the correct answers with each group the first time students play using a new set of cards. Read aloud each student's cards, and then have students silently read their cards at least five times to build fluency. Discuss each question and corresponding answer so students can concentrate more on reading fluently than on determining the answer to the question as they play.

4. Tell the group that the student who has the clue card that says *I have the first card* will begin the game by reading aloud his or her card. After the first card is read aloud, have the student with the answer to the clue read aloud his or her card. Tell students to continue until they get back to the first card. (The game ends after a student reads *Who has the first card?* and a student answers *I have the first card.*)

5. Encourage students to play the game at least twice. Have them mix up the cards and pass the cards out again so that students read different cards each time.

Extension

Invite students to take home a set of cards. Have them teach their family how to play and practice reading the cards with family members. Encourage families to make additional cards.

Synonyms

I have   the first card.

Who has the word that means   the same as **unsafe**?

I have   the word **risky**.

Who has the word that means   the same as **stop**?

I have   the word **halt**.

Who has the word that means   the same as **trip**?

I have   the word **journey**.

Who has the word that means   the same as **carry**?

I have   the word **tote**.

Who has the word that means   the same as **enemy**?

I have   the word **foe**.

Who has the word that means   the same as **alone**?

Developing Reading Fluency • Gr. 4 © 2003 Creative Teaching Press

Read-Arounds

Synonyms

I have   the word **isolated**.

Who has the word that means   the same as **many**?

I have   the word **numerous**.

Who has the word that means   the same as **jealous**?

I have   the word **envious**.

Who has the word that means   the same as **splendid**?

I have   the word **magnificent**.

Who has the word that means   the same as **ready**?

I have   the word **prepared**.

Who has the word that means   the same as **polite**?

I have   the word **courteous**.

Who has   the first card?

Developing Reading Fluency • Gr. 4 © 2003 Creative Teaching Press

Antonyms

I have   the first card.

Who has the word that means   the opposite of **alert**?

I have   the word **unaware**.

Who has the word that means   the opposite of **strange**?

I have   the word **ordinary**.

Who has the word that means   the opposite of **feeble**?

I have   the word **powerful**.

Who has the word that means   the opposite of **positive**?

I have   the word **negative**.

Who has the word that means   the opposite of **division**?

I have   the word **multiplication**.

Who has the word that means   the opposite of **elderly**?

Developing Reading Fluency • Gr. 4 © 2003 Creative Teaching Press

Read-Arounds

Antonyms

I have   the word **youthful**.

Who has the word that means   the opposite of **orderly**?

I have   the word **untidy**.

Who has the word that means   the opposite of **active**?

I have   the word **dormant**.

Who has the word that means   the opposite of **clever**?

I have   the word **foolish**.

Who has the word that means   the opposite of **bored**?

I have   the word **excited**.

Who has the word that means   the opposite of **cozy**?

I have   the word **uncomfortable**.

Who has   the first card?

Developing Reading Fluency • Gr. 4 © 2003 Creative Teaching Press

Prefixes

I have   the first card.

Who has the name   of the **meaningful chunk**

that goes at the front of a word   **to change the meaning?**

I have   the word **prefix**.

Who has the name   of the **meaningful chunk**

that goes at the end of a word   **to change the meaning?**

I have   the word **suffix**.

Who has the prefix   that means **life?**

I have   the prefix **bio-**.

Who has the prefix   that means **not?**

I have   the prefix **un-**.

Who has the prefix   that means **three?**

I have   the prefix **tri-**.

Who has the prefix   that means **around?**

Developing Reading Fluency • Gr. 4 © 2003 Creative Teaching Press

Prefixes

I have   the prefix **circum-**.

Who has the prefix   that means **under**?

I have   the prefix **sub-**.

Who has the prefix   that means **half**?

I have   the prefix **semi-**.

Who has the prefix   that means **out**?

I have   the prefix **ex-**.

Who has the prefix   that means **with**?

I have   the prefix **co-**.

Who has the prefix   that means **earth**?

I have   the prefix **geo-**.

Who has the prefix   that means **badly or abnormal**?

I have   the prefix **mal-**.

Who has   the first card?

Developing Reading Fluency • Gr. 4 © 2003 Creative Teaching Press

Grammar and Writing Terms

I have   the first card.

Who has the **type of story**   **that uses humor and exaggeration to tell unbelievable stories?**

I have   the **tall tale.**

Who has the **type of story   that often has an element of magic and sometimes teaches a lesson?**

I have   the **folktale.**

Who has the **type of writing   that tells the reader about a specific topic to teach something?**

I have   **informative writing.**

Who has the **type of writing   that tells the reader about something that really happened to you?**

I have   the **personal narrative.**

Who has the **type of writing   that has a headline, a lead paragraph, and a body?**

Grammar and Writing Terms

I have   the **news story**.

Who has the **type of writing**   in which you try

to influence someone's opinion?

I have   **persuasive writing**.

Who has the **step in the writing process**   when you plan

what you will write   and you gather information?

I have   the **prewriting step**.

Who has the **step in the writing process**

when you share your writing   with someone else

after the revising and editing is done?

I have   the **publishing step**.

Who has the **step in the writing process**   when you check

to make sure   that you used capital letters and punctuation?

I have   the **editing step**.

Who has the **step in the writing process**   when you check

to make sure   that your writing sounds good   and you make

word changes to make it better?

Developing Reading Fluency • Gr. 4 © 2003 Creative Teaching Press

Grammar and Writing Terms

I have   the **revising step**.

Who has the **word in a sentence**   that is a **person, place, or thing**?

I have   the **noun**.

Who has the **word in a sentence**   that **shows the action**?

I have   the **verb**.

Who has the **word in a sentence**   that **describes the noun to help the reader or listener   picture the sentence better**?

I have   the **adjective**.

Who has the **word**   that **describes a verb in a sentence**?

I have   the **adverb**.

Who has the **mark you would write**   at the **end of a sentence that asks a question**?

I have   the **question mark**.

Who has the **mark you would write**   at the **end of a sentence that shows surprise or excitement**?

I have   the **exclamation point**.

Who has the name of the **word**   that is **used to combine two sentences into one**?

I have   the **conjunction**.

Who has   the **first card**?

Developing Reading Fluency • Gr. 4 © 2003 Creative Teaching Press

Read-Arounds

Mathematical Vocabulary

I have   the first card.

Who has the term   that is defined as

lines that never intersect?

I have   **parallel lines.**

Who has the term   that is defined as

two lines that intersect   to form right angles?

I have   **perpendicular lines.**

Who has the term   that is defined as   an **angle with a measure**

that is less than that of a right angle   (less than 90 degrees)?

I have   the **acute angle.**

Who has the term   that is defined as   the **average, which is found**

by dividing the sum of a group of numbers

by the number of addends?

I have   the **mean.**

Who has the term   that is defined as

the **distance around a figure?**

I have   the **perimeter.**

Who has the term   that is defined as

the **chance of an event occurring?**

Developing Reading Fluency • Gr. 4 © 2003 Creative Teaching Press

Mathematical Vocabulary

I have **probability**.

Who has the term that is defined as the **number below the bar in a fraction**?

I have the **denominator**.

Who has the term that is defined as **the distance around a circle**?

I have the **circumference**.

Who has the term that is defined as a **segment that connects the center of a circle to any point on the circle**?

I have the **radius**.

Who has the term that is defined as **a simple closed plane figure made up of three or more line segments**?

I have a **polygon**.

Who has the term that is defined as the **answer to a division problem**?

I have the **quotient**.

Who has the first card?

Read-Arounds

Science Concepts

I have   the first card.

Who has the name   of the **steps in a science experiment**?

I have   the **procedure**.

Who has the name   of the **educated guess**

based on scientific knowledge

that is made in the beginning of an experiment?

I have   the **hypothesis**.

Who has the **section of an experiment**

in which you record your information   in tables, charts, or lists?

I have   the **results**.

Who has the **unit of measurement**   by which mass is measured

in a scientific experiment?

I have   **grams**.

Who has the term   for **anything used in an experiment**

that can be changed or kept the same?

I have   the **variable**.

Who has the scientific term   for **information**?

Developing Reading Fluency • Gr. 4 © 2003 Creative Teaching Press

Science Concepts

I have   the word **data**.

Who has the word   that describes **how temperature is measured**?

I have   **degrees Fahrenheit or Celsius**.

Who has the **unit of measure**   by which **liquid capacity is measured**?

I have   **milliliters**.

Who has the name   of the **container used

to measure liquids in milliliters**?

I have   the **graduated cylinder**.

Who has   the **three states of matter**?

I have   **solid, liquid, and gas**.

Who has   the **path through which electricity travels**?

I have   a **circuit**.

Who has   the first card?

Developing Reading Fluency • Gr. 4 © 2003 Creative Teaching Press

Plays for Two

Reading is a social event. People who enjoy books like to talk about them and recommend their favorite books. In classrooms, students are often asked to read alone. However, reading with a partner helps students develop phrasing and fluency through repeated oral reading while incorporating the social aspect of reading. Each Plays for Two story is designed for a pair of students to read together. Students will read their parts many times (repeated oral reading strategy) to improve their phrasing and fluency. Then, they will give a final reading for another pair, you, or the whole class. This activity helps reading take on a purpose.

Strategies: repeated oral reading, paired reading

Materials
- notebook/clear notebook sheet protectors

Directions
1. Make two single-sided copies of a paired reading script for each pair of students. (Each script is two pages long.) Do not copy the pages back-to-back. The print bleeds through and is visually distracting to students.
2. Divide the class into pairs. Give each pair a set of scripts.
3. Introduce the text to each pair through guided reading. Then, give partners time to practice reading together. (Have students practice reading and rereading many times to help them develop phrasing and fluency.)
4. To help students develop oral language and public speaking skills in front of a group, invite partners to "perform" their reading in front of the class or for a small group.
5. Train students to give each other specific compliments on their performance. Have them use the words and phrases *sounds like talking, phrasing,* and *fluent.*
6. Store each paired reading script in a clear notebook sheet protector (front to back). Store the sheet protectors in a notebook to make them easily accessible for future use.

Extension
Invite students to make cutouts of the characters and objects in the story to make it more interactive. Have students color the cutouts and glue them to craft sticks to use as props.

Reader's Theater

Reader's Theater is a motivating and exciting way for students to mature into fluent and expressive readers. Reader's Theater does not use any props, costumes, or materials other than the script, which allows the focus to stay on fluent and expressive reading. The "actors" must tell the story by using only their voices and must rely on their tone of voice, expression, phrasing, and fluency to express the story to the audience. Students are reading for a purpose, which highly motivates them because they take on the roles of characters and bring the characters to life through voice inflection. Each Reader's Theater script is designed for a group of four students. However, the scripts can be modified, if necessary. For example, students can double-up on roles to incorporate paired reading.

Strategies: repeated oral reading model for groups of four, choral reading, paired reading

Materials
- highlighters
- colored file folders
- sentence strips
- yarn

Directions

1. Make four copies of each play. (Each play is several pages long.) Staple together the pages along the left side of the script (not the top). Highlight a different character's part in each script.
2. Gather four folders of the same color for each play. Put one copy of the script in each folder. Write the title of the play and the name of the highlighted character (e.g., Falling Asleep, Tom) on the front of each folder.
3. Divide the class into groups of four. Give each student in a group a folder of the same color (containing the same script).
4. Have students first read the entire script. (Research supports having students read all of the roles for the first day or two to fully comprehend the story.) Then, have students choose which part they will perform, or assign each student a part. Have students switch folders so that each student has the script with the highlighted character's part that he or she will play.
5. Write each character's name on a sentence strip to make name tags. Hole-punch the name tags, and tie yarn through the holes. Give each student a name tag to wear. Have students spend at least four to five days reading and rereading their part to practice phrasing and fluency.
6. Invite students to perform their play for the whole class, another group, a buddy class, or their parents.

Extension

Invite more advanced readers to choose a script and put on a puppet show with a group. (This type of performance is dramatic play, not Reader's Theater, because students use props with their voices to tell the story.) Invite the group to practice their lines, make puppets (out of paper bags, toilet paper rolls, or craft sticks), and perform the play.

The Club

Theme: character education–fairness

Characters: Narrator Keisha
Luca Fran

Narrator

Have you ever been in a club? Did you join it or make it up yourself? Did you let anybody join? Were there rules? Were they fair? This is what happened one day at recess. Maybe you've seen something like this happen at recess, too.

Luca

I'm starting a club! Only people who have brown hair can be in my club. I won't let anyone else in. If I don't like you, then you can't be in my club either.

Narrator

Luca was saying this to a group of people he usually played with at school. They were third through fifth graders.

Keisha

Who gets to be in it? Boys or girls?

Luca

That doesn't matter as long as you have brown hair.

Fran

I have brown hair. Can I be in your club?

Luca

Sure! Who else wants to be in my club?

Keisha

I have brown hair. Can I be in your club?

Developing Reading Fluency • Gr. 4 © 2003 Creative Teaching Press

The Club

Luca

Sure! Who else wants to be in my club?

Narrator

Lindsay and Christian came over. They said that they didn't have brown hair, but they were in every school club.

Luca

No way! You have blond hair. You can't be in our club. This is only for people who have brown hair.

Fran

But Lindsay is my best friend. I want her to be in our club.

Luca

You knew this was a brown-haired club when you joined. Lindsay has blond hair, so she doesn't fit in. She can't be in our club!

Fran

Well, I don't know if I want to be in a club if my best friend can't be in it, too.

Luca

Too bad! You decide. Only people with brown hair are in. We're going to have a clubhouse, posters, and parties. You're going to miss out if you decide not to be in the club.

Narrator

Fran thought about that for a minute. She looked at Lindsay. She looked at Christian. Christian didn't care so he walked off. He had plenty of other friends. Lindsay started to cry. Fran thought of the parties and the clubhouse. She had always wanted to be in a club with a clubhouse.

Developing Reading Fluency • Gr. 4 © 2003 Creative Teaching Press

Reader's Theater

The Club

Keisha

Can my best friend, Mia, be in our club? She has brown hair, too.

Luca

Sure! Okay, we have enough people. Let's plan what we are going to do. I think we should make a club flag at our first meeting. We could all meet at my house after school, since I live right across the street. My mom will make cake and punch. We'll plan our first party at that meeting.

Keisha

What kinds of things will our club do? My sister is in a club and they sell cookies, wash cars, and collect cans at every holiday to give to families who need assistance. What will we do?

Luca

We're too cool for all of that! We will have parties, talk about other people, and decide who our friends will be.

Narrator

Keisha and Fran looked at each other. Fran still couldn't decide what to do. She really wanted to have the cake and punch. She wanted to be Luca's friend, since he was the most popular boy in her class. She wanted to be in a club so badly.

Keisha

Wait a minute! You mean to tell me that we're only going to eat, talk about people, and plan parties? That's not for me! I want to do something that matters. I want to help other people.

Developing Reading Fluency • Gr. 4 © 2003 Creative Teaching Press

The Club

Fran

Yes, and I've been thinking about it. I don't think it's fair to have a club with people who look a certain way. I don't want to be part of your silly old club.

Luca

Of course you do! I'm the most popular kid in school. If you're in my club, then you'll be popular, too.

Fran

That's crazy! You keep your club. I'm going to keep my friends.

Keisha

You keep up that attitude of yours and you won't have any friends left. Who has ever heard of having a club with only people who have brown hair? Anyone could dye their hair anyway. I agree with Fran! You keep your club!

Luca

You'll be sorry!

Narrator *(asking the audience one question at a time)*

Do you think Fran and Keisha made the right decision?
Did they regret it?
What do you think happened next?
What would you do?

Developing Reading Fluency • Gr. 4 © 2003 Creative Teaching Press

Reader's Theater

Falling Asleep

Theme: friendship

Characters: Narrator   Tom

                 Keith   Mom

Narrator

Have you ever had a hard time falling asleep? Did you try counting sheep? Perhaps you tried thinking about something you enjoy doing. Well, Tom was having this same problem while he was spending the night at Keith's house.

Tom

Keith, are you asleep?

Keith

No, I can't seem to fall asleep. Do you want to watch TV until we fall asleep?

Tom

That sounds like a good idea. Do you think your mom will say that we can? She told us that we had to be in bed by 10:00 tonight if I slept over. Now we're in bed, but we can't fall asleep!

Keith

I think that the TV will help us fall asleep, so I think she'll agree to let us watch it. M-ooo-m!

Mom

Did you call me? I thought you boys were fast asleep by now. It's almost 10:45. What are you boys doing up?

Tom and Keith

We can't sleep.

Keith

We're trying, but it's not working.

Developing Reading Fluency • Gr. 4 © 2003 Creative Teaching Press

Falling Asleep

Mom

Did you try reading your books until your eyes got more tired?

Tom

We did! Honest! We still can't fall asleep.

Keith

We were thinking that if we could watch a little bit of TV, then we could fall asleep.

Tom

Right now, I'm just lying here thinking about the state report I have to write that's due next Friday. That's keeping me awake.

Mom

You should try counting sheep. That always helps me fall asleep.

Keith

Come on, Mom! We're not going to count sheep.

Mom

Well then, count monsters! I know you like monsters. Whatever it takes to get you boys to fall asleep. Tom, I promised your dad that you'd get to sleep at a decent hour so you wouldn't be tired at your soccer game tomorrow.

Tom

I know. It's just that we would probably fall asleep if we watched a tiny bit of TV. I always go to bed with the TV on at home.

Mom

Well, I'll agree to 15 minutes of TV. Then, I'm coming in to turn it off. Now you boys need to get to sleep!

Developing Reading Fluency • Gr. 4 © 2003 Creative Teaching Press

Reader's Theater

Falling Asleep

Keith

Will you at least consider a half hour so that we can see an entire show? Otherwise, you'll turn it off in the middle of a show and we'll probably lie here thinking about how it would have ended.

Mom

Well, that does make sense. Okay! You boys can watch TV until 11:30, but no talking. I want you to try your best to fall asleep.

Keith

Thanks Mom! We promise!

Narrator

Keith started flipping through the channels. The first show was a cooking show.

Tom

I love cooking shows! Let's watch that.

Keith

We can find something better than that. I think that there's a monster marathon on tonight. Let's keep looking.

Narrator

The next channel Keith flipped to was a home shopping channel.

Tom

No way! Not that!

Narrator

The next channel had an old black-and-white show about a husband and wife who lived in an apartment. Their best friends owned the building.

Developing Reading Fluency • Gr. 4 © 2003 Creative Teaching Press

Falling Asleep

Tom

That's my mom's favorite show! Let's watch the end and see what comes on at 11:00.

Keith

My mom loves this show, too! I think Lucy is just like my mom.

Narrator

The boys watched as Lucy went shopping to buy a dress, found out the dresses were very expensive, and bought a simple black one.

Tom

Doesn't your mom have a dress like that?

Keith

My mom loves to shop. She has so many black dresses!

Narrator

They continued watching as Lucy wore the dress in a fashion show in order to keep it for free. She had a bad sunburn, so she walked funny in the fashion show. Both boys started laughing.

Tom

Why would anyone want to be in a fashion show?

Keith

I have no idea!

Narrator

Just then, the door opened.

Mom

All right boys! You're supposed to be falling asleep. Every time I walk by the door I hear you talking. Do I need to turn off the TV and put you in separate rooms?

Developing Reading Fluency • Gr. 4 © 2003 Creative Teaching Press

Reader's Theater

Falling Asleep

Tom and Keith
NO!

Keith
We're sorry! We were watching your favorite show and we started talking about it. We promise to lay here quietly and watch TV until we fall asleep.

Tom
We promise.

Mom
This is your last chance. Good night boys! Sweet dreams!

Tom
Let's see if we can find that monster marathon now.

Narrator
Keith flipped through the stations and finally found it. A new show was beginning, so they were just in time.

Keith
Here it is!

Narrator
They started watching it and fell asleep. Keith's mom entered the room at 11:30.

Mom *(whispering to herself)*
Well, it's about time!

Narrator
She turned off the TV, blew kisses to both boys, and went to sleep. Meanwhile, both boys had dreams about monsters. Luckily, they weren't scary dreams!

Developing Reading Fluency • Gr. 4 © 2003 Creative Teaching Press

The Magic Television

Theme: fantasy

Characters: Narrator   Dave
                Sandra   Darren

Narrator

Have you ever wished that you could become one of the characters
on television? I don't mean the actor or actress. I mean really live
that life instead of your own. Well, this is a story of a boy who
had that wish and it suddenly came true. He learned the hard way
what was meant by the saying, "Be careful what you wish for!"

Dave

Do you both want to come over to my house after school today?
My mom just got a new TV.

Sandra

I want to, but I have to ask my parents first.

Darren

Let me check with my mom and I'll let you know.

Narrator

The next day, Sandra and Darren told Dave that they could go to
his house on Friday after school as long as they were home by
dinnertime.

Dave

Terrific! Wait until you see our new TV! It's huge!

Narrator

Friday arrived and they all had lunch at school. They talked about
what they wanted to do after school at Dave's house.

Reader's Theater

Developing Reading Fluency • Gr. 4 © 2003 Creative Teaching Press

The Magic Television

Sandra

I think we should ride our bikes. We could get an ice-cream cone and play volleyball at the park.

Darren

I think we should play basketball at the park. I saw the basketball game on TV last night and I want to try a few new moves.

Dave

I really want you both to see my TV. At first, I wanted you to see it because it was big and cool, but now I have a different reason. *(lowering his voice)* I think our new TV is magic!

Sandra

You're just being lazy. You just don't want to ride bikes, play volleyball, or play basketball.

Dave

I'm not kidding!

Darren

You're crazy! *(lowering his voice)* A TV can't be magic. It's electronic, not magic!

Dave

I can prove it! If it's not true, then I promise to ride bikes with you to the park. I'll play volleyball AND basketball!

Narrator

Sandra looked at Darren and said . . .

Sandra

How much time should we give him after school to prove it, before we go to the park with or without him?

Developing Reading Fluency • Gr. 4 © 2003 Creative Teaching Press

The Magic Television

Darren

We'll give you a half hour to prove your TV is MAGIC. After that, it's basketball time!

Sandra

You mean volleyball time.

Darren

We'll worry about that later. In any case, you have a half hour before we leave for the park.

Dave

It's a deal! Get ready to be shocked! Let's meet at my house after school.

Narrator

At the end of the day, they all met at Dave's house.

Dave

Come on! You won't believe this! I think I'm the only one who has figured this out. Otherwise, I'm sure my mom would have traded this TV in for another one by now.

Narrator

They all walked into the family room.

Sandra

That's the biggest TV I've ever seen!

Darren

Me, too! That must have cost your mom a fortune!

Dave

That's not the point. Wait until you see what it can do.

Developing Reading Fluency • Gr. 4 © 2003 Creative Teaching Press

Reader's Theater

The Magic Television

Narrator

Just then, Darren pulled out his stopwatch.

Darren

Okay, you have 30 minutes to convince us that your TV is magic. On your mark, get set, go!

Dave

That's just silly that you're really going to time me, but okay. Come sit down over here. I'll tell you how I figured it out in the first place.

Narrator

Dave told his friends that he was watching his favorite show when the characters went swimming in the ocean. They got to swim with a dolphin.

Dave

I was pushing the menu button on the remote control at the same time that I said, "I wish that was my life!" and before you know it, I was swimming with the dolphin!

Narrator

As you could well imagine, Sandra and Darren started laughing at him. They thought that was the craziest thing they had ever heard.

Darren

Get real, Dave! Let's go play basketball. I only have until 6:00 and it's already 3:35!

Sandra

Dave, you really are a comedian! Let's get going!

Developing Reading Fluency • Gr. 4 © 2003 Creative Teaching Press

The Magic Television

Dave

I'm totally serious! You just have to listen. I tried it over and over again until I figured out that it was a combination of what I said and pushing the menu button on the remote control that made the magic happen. I can prove it! I've done it four times already! I've been swimming with the dolphins, riding on a roller coaster, building sand castles in Florida, and camping in a forest. It's true!

Narrator

He sounded so convincing that they stopped laughing and looked at each other.

Darren

Well, I guess we could give you the 23 minutes you still have on my stopwatch.

Sandra

Okay, prove it. Turn on the TV and take us somewhere else.

Dave

First, I need to get the remote control. I think that since we all want to go, we will all have to have our fingers on the menu button. When I tried it on another button, it didn't work. We'll stack our fingers and say, "I wish that was my life!" all together on the count of three.

Sandra

Where are we going to go?

Dave

That depends on what show we turn on. Let's see what's on right now.

Sandra

What if your dad comes in? What if we get caught?

Developing Reading Fluency • Gr. 4 © 2003 Creative Teaching Press

Reader's Theater

The Magic Television

Dave

That's the strangest thing of all. Time didn't go by while I was gone. The clock said the same time as it did when I left!

Darren

This is sounding crazier and crazier by the minute!

Narrator

Dave was looking through the television schedule when he said . . .

Dave

Since you want to play basketball so badly, how would you like to be at this game?

Narrator

Dave showed Darren the schedule. It indicated that Darren's favorite professional basketball team was playing another team on TV at that very moment.

Dave

We can become part of the audience at that game and see it in person.

Darren

No way!

Sandra

That's impossible!

Dave

Watch! Are you ready? Let's stack our fingers on this menu button. Good. Now, on the count of three you know what to do. One, two, three . . .

Developing Reading Fluency • Gr. 4 © 2003 Creative Teaching Press

The Magic Television

Darren, Sandra, and Dave
I wish that was my life!

Narrator
Sure enough, they were suddenly sitting in the front row watching that exact basketball game! Darren and Sandra were so shocked that they didn't say a word for at least 10 minutes. Then, Darren broke the silence.

Darren
Is this a dream? Am I really here?

Sandra
I know I'm here and you're right next to me.

Darren
Are we really sitting in the front row of the same basketball game we were just watching on TV? That's impossible!

Sandra
I know it's impossible, but we're here! I can't believe it myself.

Dave
I told you! I know it seems like we must all be crazy, but we really are here! It's that TV!

Darren
How long can we stay here before your dad finds out that we aren't home?

Sandra
I don't want to get in trouble. My parents will punish me.

Developing Reading Fluency • Gr. 4 © 2003 Creative Teaching Press

Reader's Theater

The Magic Television

Dave

You don't have anything to worry about. Since time doesn't move while we're away, it will be the exact same time when we return as it was when we left. No one will even know we were gone!

Sandra

Unbelievable!

Darren

Impossible!

Dave

Unbelievable and impossible, but absolutely true! Let's enjoy the game!

Darren

How do we get back?

Dave

It's simple. All we do is say the words "I wish I could go back home" at the same time as we push down the menu button on the remote control.

Narrator

Just then, everyone started looking around. Then they began looking a bit worried. The other people in the audience, who were enjoying the game, were getting bothered by them as they looked under seats, on the floor, and behind them. Then, Dave said . . .

Dave

Where's the remote control?!?!?!?!

Developing Reading Fluency • Gr. 4 © 2003 Creative Teaching Press

The Guest Speaker

Themes: realistic fiction, science

Characters: Narrator   Dr. Shuman
Ms. Bead   Sydney

Narrator

Picture yourself in Ms. Bead's fourth-grade classroom. The students are very well behaved and always respectful. They are learning about the human body. Today, Ms. Bead has invited Sydney's dad into the classroom to teach them about the heart.

Ms. Bead

Are we going to have fun in science today! We are so lucky to have Sydney's dad here to teach us about the heart. Sydney, would you like to introduce your dad?

Sydney

Sure! Well, you already know that my dad is a famous cardiologist. He does surgery on people's hearts. You can all call him Dr. Shuman.

Ms. Bead

Can you tell us why he came here today, Sydney?

Sydney

My dad is going to teach us about the four chambers of the heart. Then, he is going to help us investigate a cow's heart that he ordered from the grocery store for us.

Ms. Bead

Let's please welcome Dr. Shuman! Thank you so much for coming to our class today to help us learn about the heart. We are so excited!

The Guest Speaker

Narrator

Dr. Shuman walked up to the front of the room with a stethoscope around his neck. He lifted it up.

Dr. Shuman

Thank you for inviting me to visit today. Does anyone know what this is?

Narrator

Sydney raised her hand first.

Dr. Shuman

Anyone other than Sydney?

Narrator

Four other children raised their hands. He called on them. They all knew that it was used to listen to the heart and lungs.

Dr. Shuman

Good! Today we are going to learn a little more about our amazing hearts! You already know what an important organ it is. I've brought some slides to show you some of the things you have been learning about.

Ms. Bead

I'll turn the lights out for you.

Narrator

She turned out the lights and Dr. Shuman began his slide presentation.

Dr. Shuman

Sydney will be my assistant, since we have practiced together at home. She will ask you to predict what is shown on each slide based on a few clues, and then I will tell you what it is and explain a bit about it. Are you ready?

Developing Reading Fluency • Gr. 4 © 2003 Creative Teaching Press

The Guest Speaker

Narrator

The class all responded with a loud "Yes!"

Sydney

What do you predict this slide is showing? Here's your clue: It's a muscle that pumps blood through your blood vessels to all parts of your body.

Narrator

Many children raised their hands and Ms. Bead chose three children to share their predictions.

Ms. Bead

I think I agree with all of you. Dr. Shuman, we know that the heart is a muscle. Is that a picture of the heart?

Dr. Shuman

Very good! Yes, it is the heart! The heart muscle is the most important part of your circulatory system. Did you know that it is only as big as your fist? Although it's small, the heart is a hard worker. The only time it stops working is when it rests between beats. This stethoscope will allow me to listen to someone's heartbeat. I can count how many times your heart beats in a minute.

Narrator

He took ten stethoscopes out of a bag.

Ms. Bead

Dr. Shuman was kind enough to bring some in for us to test. You will have a chance to work with a partner later in the week using these stethoscopes.

Developing Reading Fluency • Gr. 4 © 2003 Creative Teaching Press

The Guest Speaker

Narrator

The class got excited and Ms. Bead had to get them quiet again.

Dr. Shuman

Let's look at the next slide.

Sydney

Here's your clue: This is a close-up picture of the blood vessels that carry blood AWAY from the heart.

Ms. Bead

Remember what we learned! A-A- _____ away!

Narrator

The whole class said, "Arteries!" at the same time.

Dr. Shuman

That's right! What a clever way to remember that. How do you say it?

Narrator

The class said, "A-A-Arteries away!" Ms. Bead was smiling. You could tell that she was proud.

Dr. Shuman

Very clever! Yes, this is a picture of someone's arteries. As you can see from the next few pictures of the arteries, they branch out to all parts of your body. It is important to eat a healthy diet, so that your arteries don't get clogged.

Sydney

Do you mean clogged like a drain?

Developing Reading Fluency • Gr. 4 © 2003 Creative Teaching Press

The Guest Speaker

Dr. Shuman

That's a good comparison. In your mind, picture your kitchen sink. What happens when the sink gets clogged? That's right, the water doesn't go down very well. It's the same thing with your arteries. If they get clogged due to eating unhealthy fatty foods, then the blood can't flow through very easily. This can lead to heart disease and other heart problems.

Ms. Bead

That's why it's so important to eat balanced meals like we learned when we studied the food pyramid.

Dr. Shuman

So, the arteries are very important to protect since they carry blood to all parts of your body. Let's look at the next picture.

Sydney

Here's your clue for this picture: You probably think of them as the opposite of arteries.

Narrator

The whole class said, "Veins!" at the same time.

Dr. Shuman

Very good! Yes, these are veins. They aren't exactly the opposite of arteries, but they do flow in the opposite direction. They are the blood vessels responsible for carrying blood to your heart. Let's look at the next slide.

Sydney

This picture is showing what the arteries become as they get smaller and smaller.

Developing Reading Fluency • Gr. 4 © 2003 Creative Teaching Press

The Guest Speaker

Ms. Bead
We haven't learned about those yet, so you will get to teach us something new.

Dr. Shuman
Terrific! This is a picture of capillaries. As the arteries branch out to other parts of your body, they get smaller and smaller. They eventually turn into capillaries. The capillaries are tiny little blood vessels that then carry the blood to every cell in your body.

Sydney
This last picture shows the four parts (or chambers) of something we started off talking about.

Ms. Bead
We know this one class. What is that?

Narrator
They all said, "The heart!"

Dr. Shuman
That's right. This is a picture of a heart. It's not a real picture like the others, but it clearly shows you the four chambers of the heart. This is the left atrium, the right atrium, the left ventricle, and the right ventricle. I've brought a surprise for all of you to investigate today.

Ms. Bead
You are going to have so much fun exploring and comparing what we know about a human heart with . . .

Developing Reading Fluency • Gr. 4 © 2003 Creative Teaching Press

The Guest Speaker

Sydney
A cow's heart!

Narrator
Throughout the class, you could hear a mixture of "Ewwwww!" and "Cool!"

Ms. Bead
Dr. Shuman was kind enough to special order two cow hearts for us to investigate. These are real cow hearts!

Dr. Shuman
The cow heart is very similar to the human heart, although much larger. You will be able to investigate the four chambers. You will even be able to see some arteries and veins!

Ms. Bead
What do we say to Dr. Shuman for teaching us about the heart, bringing in slides and stethoscopes, and donating the cow hearts?

Narrator
The class said, "Thank you" and then gave him some compliments. Later that day, they went over to the science investigation table to investigate the cow hearts. They got to feel around inside each cow heart. Would you do that?

Phrasing Memory Challenges

Students who are still not reading with phrasing and fluency will have a difficult time with the transition from learning to read to reading to learn, since their comprehension will be significantly impaired. Students who lack phrasing and fluency will be "word reading" rather than reading for meaning. These students need many opportunities to listen to phrasing, practice reading phrased chunks of three to four words, and transfer this practice into ongoing text. The fun, motivating memory challenges in this section provide modeling and practice, while challenging students' auditory memory for phrased units. This puts the emphasis on meaning rather than decoding. As the challenge to add a new word or phrase continues, the sentence becomes longer. The phrases themselves change along the way as well, which helps students understand that phrased chunks hold meaning. Each challenge was designed to be used one-on-one between a teacher and a student or as a peer coaching tool between a fluent reader and a less-fluent reader. By reading in phrases and then building on the phrases, the student practices fluency. The application of these strategies to nonfiction text is key, since many students can read fluently in fiction but sound choppy when reading nonfiction.

Strategies: modeled reading, echo reading, repeated oral reading, meaningful chunks, transfer to nonfiction

Materials
- no additional materials are required

Directions

1. Choose a memory challenge, and make one copy of the reproducible.
2. Sit facing the student. (NOTE: You could also have a peer tutor work with the student.)
3. Begin by reading the first sentence. Tell the student to echo (repeat) the first line using his or her auditory memory of the phrases. (The student does not have a copy of the text.)
4. Then, read the second sentence. (Each line adds an additional word or phrase to the original sentence. In some cases, the sentence is slightly revised to incorporate the new text. This teaches the student that a phrase is a meaningful chunk of words rather than a set number of words read together.) Tell the student to echo the sentence.
5. Continue to model reading the remaining sentences on the reproducible, and invite the student to echo each line.
6. Switch roles with the student, and invite him or her to take the role of the teacher and read the first sentence. Repeat the process of modeling and echoing as described in steps 3–5.
7. Then, ask the student to read the nonfiction paragraph at the bottom of the reproducible. This text begins with the complete sentence the student just practiced. This part of the activity provides the transfer process to reading nonfiction text fluently.

Extension

Incorporate choral reading (teacher and student reading together) into this activity for students who have difficulty reading the nonfiction paragraph at the bottom of the page.

The Rabbit

I see a rabbit.

I see   a big rabbit.

I see   a big, furry rabbit.

I see   a big, furry rabbit   on the grass.

I see   a big, furry rabbit   on the grass   eating dandelion leaves.

I see   a big, furry rabbit   on the grass   eating dandelion leaves
on a sunny day.

I see   a big, furry rabbit   on the grass   eating dandelion leaves
on a sunny day   in the middle of summer.

I see a big, furry rabbit on the grass eating dandelion leaves on a sunny day in the middle of summer. Contrary to what you usually see in cartoons, rabbits do not like carrots the best. Rabbits prefer eating dandelion leaves, alfalfa, and spinach. Rabbits do like to eat carrots, but they like the tops and green vegetables even more. Rabbits must eat all of these fresh foods to stay healthy.

Phrasing Memory Challenges

Layers of Earth

This is Earth.

This is the crust   of Earth.

This is the mantle   under the crust   of Earth.

This is the outer core   under the mantle,   which is under the crust of Earth.

This is the outer core   made partly of liquid,   which is under the mantle, which is under the crust   of Earth.

This is the outer core made partly of liquid, which is under the mantle, which is under the crust of Earth. The inner core, which is the center of Earth, is made up of iron. Therefore, from the inside out, Earth is made up of the inner core, outer core, mantle, and crust. The crust is made up of rock. It is very thin in comparison to the other layers of Earth. The mantle is another layer of rock. There has not been anyone who has made it to the mantle, since it is very hot. Lava that comes to Earth's surface from a volcano comes from the magma of the mantle.

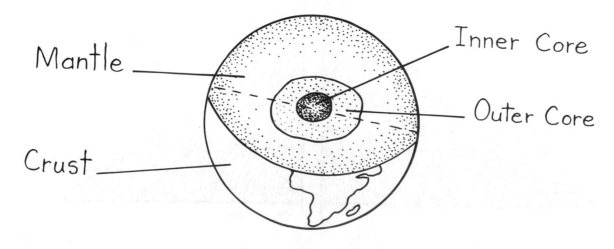

Volcanoes

Can you see   the volcano?

Can you see   the volcano   formed by lava?

Can you see   the volcano   formed by lava and ash?

Can you see   the composite volcano   formed by lava and ash?

Can you see   the tall composite volcano   formed by lava and ash?

Can you see   the tall composite volcano,   which is fairly steep,
formed by lava and ash?

Can you see the tall composite volcano, which is fairly steep, formed by lava and ash? There are three main types of volcanoes: shield, cinder cone, and composite. Although composite volcanoes are made of lava and ash, the shield volcanoes are mostly lava. The cinder cone volcanoes are mostly ash. Volcanoes take on their shape as the lava and ash build up around the openings.

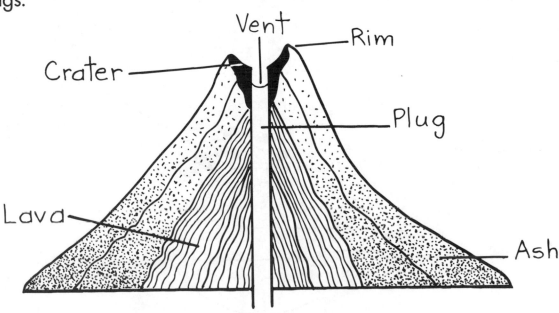

Phrasing Memory Challenges

Food Chain

This is the grass.

This is the grass   at the bottom   of the food chain.

This is the grasshopper   that eats the grass   at the bottom
of the food chain.

This is the snake   that eats the grasshopper   that eats the grass
at the bottom   of the food chain.

This is the hawk   that eats the snake   that eats the grasshopper
that eats the grass   at the bottom   of the food chain.

This is the hawk that eats the snake that eats the grasshopper that eats the grass at the bottom of the food chain. A food chain shows how all living things are connected to each other based on what they eat. Every link in the food chain is important. If one living thing becomes extinct, then all other living things that rely upon it for food will be in danger.

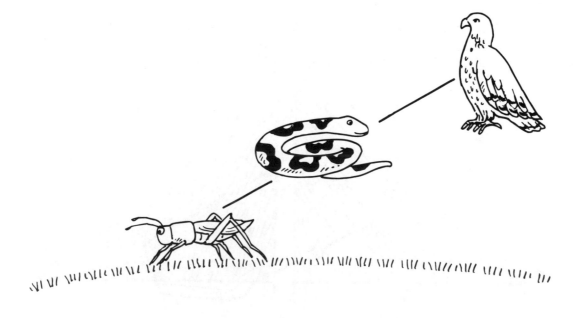

Developing Reading Fluency • Gr. 4 © 2003 Creative Teaching Press

The Gold Rush

This is gold.

This is   a gold nugget.

This is   a gold nugget   found in a gold mine.

This is   a gold nugget   found in a gold mine   in California.

This is   a gold nugget   found in a gold mine   in 1848 in California.

This is   a gold nugget   found in a gold mine   in 1848 in California
by James Marshall.

This is   a gold nugget   found in a gold mine   in 1848 in California
by James Marshall   at Sutter's Mill.

This is a gold nugget found in a gold mine in 1848 in California by James Marshall at Sutter's Mill. He is credited with beginning the California Gold Rush, during which many people traveled west in hopes of becoming rich. People also came from as far away as Europe, China, and Australia. Violence and crime became a problem as new settlers entered California. California wrote a constitution to create laws and became a state in 1850.

Developing Reading Fluency • Gr. 4 © 2003 Creative Teaching Press

Phrasing Memory Challenges

Native Americans

This is a tribe.

This is a tribe   of Native Americans.

This is a tribe   of Native Americans   who were fishermen.

This is a tribe   of Native Americans   who were fishermen
   in the Pacific Northwest.

This is a tribe   of Native Americans   who were fishermen
   in the Pacific Northwest   along the coast.

This is a tribe   of Native Americans   who were fishermen
   relying on salmon   in the Pacific Northwest   along the coast.

This is a tribe of Native Americans who were fishermen relying on salmon in the Pacific Northwest along the coast. The tribes in this region could be divided into four groups: hunters, gatherers, fishermen, and farmers. The tribes that were fishermen built fishing platforms over a river. They fished with nets, spears, hooks, and lines. They also carved many things out of wood.

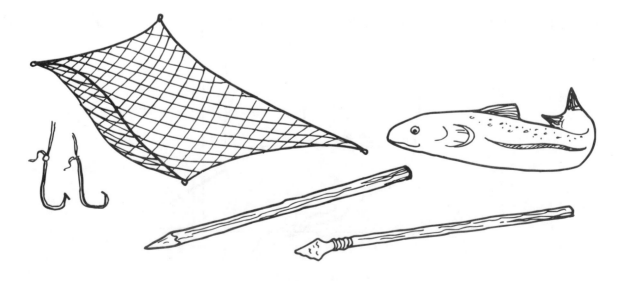

Developing Reading Fluency • Gr. 4 © 2003 Creative Teaching Press

Every section in this book can be used throughout the year to teach, guide, practice, and reinforce reading with phrasing and fluency, which will improve students' reading comprehension. The following activities provide additional practice and instruction for those students who need more help with the strategies that will help them improve their reading fluency. Assess students' stage of fluency development often by referring to the chart on page 7.

Use the following activities with "robotic readers" to help them be successful. The activities in this section will help students focus on the following strategies: phrased reading, automaticity with high-frequency words, recognition of what fluency sounds like at the listening level, and active listening.

Each activity includes an objective, a materials list, and step-by-step directions. The activities are most suited to individualized instruction or very small groups. The activities can be adapted for use with larger groups or a whole-class setting in some cases.

Phrasing Pyramids

Strategy: explicit phrasing

Objective: Each student will practice reading phrases of increasing length with fluency.

Materials
- Pyramids reproducible (page 89)

Directions

1. Give each student a Pyramids reproducible.
2. Discuss the sample in the first pyramid. Model how to read each line of increasing length as one continuous phrase. (Option: Use guided practice following the Fantastic Five Format described on page 8.)
3. Brainstorm topics that students can write about to create sentences for the blank pyramids.
4. Have each student write a sentence in the blank pyramid (using the same format as the example).
5. Read aloud each student-written pyramid to further model phrasing to the group.
6. Invite students to switch papers with a classmate and read each other's sentences.
7. Optional: Have students draw pyramids and write additional sentences.
8. Invite students to discuss what they learned by completing this activity.

Pyramids

We
We need
We need to
We need to reduce
We need to reduce, reuse
We need to reduce, reuse, and
We need to reduce, reuse, and recycle
We need to reduce, reuse, and recycle to
We need to reduce, reuse, and recycle to help
We need to reduce, reuse, and recycle to help protect
We need to reduce, reuse, and recycle to help protect our
We need to reduce, reuse, and recycle to help protect our world.

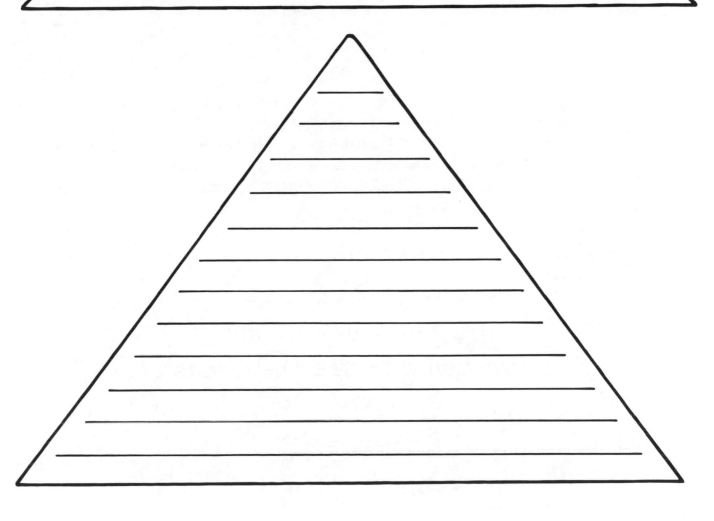

Phrasing Fun with Friends

Strategy: explicit phrasing

Objectives: Each student will understand what phrasing sounds like and looks like in text. Each student will transfer phrasing and fluency to ongoing text.

Materials
- The Art Contest 1 and 2 reproducibles (pages 91–92)
- The Aquarium 1 and 2 reproducibles (pages 93–94)
- familiar children's books

Directions

1. Copy a class set of The Art Contest 1 and 2 reproducibles.

2. Divide the class into small groups. Write in each blank the name of a student in the group you are working with.

3. Give each student a The Art Contest 1 reproducible. Read the text following the Fantastic Five Format (described on page 8).

Step 1: Model how to read each phrase.

Step 2: Echo reading—Read one phrase at a time as students repeat.

Step 3: Choral reading—Guide students as they read with phrasing.

Step 4: Independent reading—Have students read the phrases without you.

Step 5: Reverse echo reading—Have students read the phrases, and then repeat them.

---

4. Give each student a The Art Contest 2 reproducible. (It has the same phrases as reproducible 1, but it is written in an ongoing text format and has an additional paragraph of related text. This reproducible is the KEY! It is very important that you do not skip this reproducible because students will practice transferring their skills of reading phrases fluently to reading sentences in a paragraph fluently.)

5. Choral read the reproducible together. Then, invite the group to read it aloud to you.

6. Repeat the activity with The Aquarium reproducibles for further practice.

7. Invite students to practice their phrasing and fluency by reading a familiar book. Easy guided reading books are perfect.

The Art Contest 1

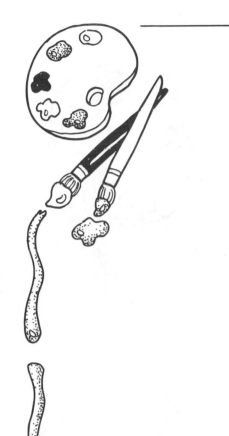

_____ and _____

were planning to be

in the art contest.

They bought crayons,

watercolor paints,

and brightly colored paper.

They drew a picture

of a large rabbit.

Then, they painted

the background

with the watercolors.

Their watercolor painting

won first prize!

Developing Reading Fluency • Gr. 4 © 2003 Creative Teaching Press

The Art Contest 2

_____ and _____ were

planning to be in the art contest. They bought crayons,

watercolor paints, and brightly colored paper.

They drew a picture of a large rabbit. Then,

they painted the background with the

watercolors. Their watercolor painting won

first prize!

Some people thought that they won first

prize because they included so much detail.

Other people said it was because the rabbit

they drew looked so realistic. In

any case, they won their school art contest.

The next step was to send their artwork to

the county fair. They were hoping that they

could win a blue ribbon for the best

watercolor portrait. Since animals were

popular at the county fair, they thought they

had a good chance. What do you

think happened?

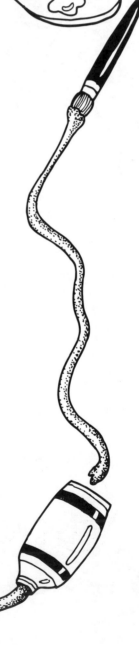

Developing Reading Fluency • Gr. 4 © 2003 Creative Teaching Press

The Aquarium 1

_____ and _____

went on a field trip

to the aquarium

with their class.

They both agreed

that their favorite creature

was the hammerhead shark.

They took pictures

of the dolphins

and the sea lions.

On the bus ride

back to school,

they talked about

the fun they had.

Developing Reading Fluency • Gr. 4 © 2003 Creative Teaching Press

Intervention Instruction

The Aquarium 2

_____ and _____ went on

a field trip to the aquarium with their class. They

both agreed that their favorite creature was

the hammerhead shark. They took pictures

of the dolphins and the sea lions. On the bus

ride back to school, they talked about the fun

they had.

As they were talking, they discovered how much

they had in common. They both loved sea

animals. They enjoyed touching the sea urchins

and manta rays the most. Although the sea stars

were interesting to look at, it was more exciting

to watch the seals swimming around in the huge

tanks of water. They talked about how they

could ask their parents for season passes to the

aquarium. In their opinion, it would be much

more fun to spend the weekends at the aquarium

than sitting around watching TV. They were sure

their parents would agree with them!

Developing Reading Fluency • Gr. 4 © 2003 Creative Teaching Press

Strategy: explicit phrasing

Objectives: Each student will understand why punctuation is so important. Each student will identify punctuation in text that is read aloud and apply this in reading and writing.

Materials
- scissors
- small index cards
- short stories or books

Directions

1. Cut small index cards in half. Give each student four cut cards.

2. Tell students to draw a period, a question mark, an exclamation point, and quotation marks on separate cards.

3. Read aloud a short story. Tell students to hold up a card to indicate the type of punctuation needed in the sentence. For example, as you change speaking voices for different characters, they will hold up the quotation marks. If you ask a question, they will hold up a question mark.

4. Explain to students that good stories have sentences that use different kinds of punctuation. They are not all simple sentences or statements.

5. Invite students to work with a partner. Have the pair take turns reading a short story or book to each other. Tell the listener to hold up the index card that indicates what he or she hears at the end of each sentence. Then, invite partners to switch roles.

6. Remind students that good readers and writers pay close attention to the punctuation clues. Encourage them to do this when they read and write.

When you see quotation marks, a person is saying dialogue.

. period
? question mark
! exclamation point
" " quotation marks

Intervention Instruction

In some severe cases, students have never moved beyond one-to-one matching of every word to speech. This usually causes students to "voice point," which sounds robotic. If a student moved into silent reading before becoming fluent, he or she will "eye point." Fluent readers see at least three to five words ahead of their speech. That's how fluent readers know when to change their voice, form a question, or act surprised. A student who reads one word at a time cannot do this, since his or her eyes only see the word being read. This activity is designed to be used daily for 3 to 5 minutes to transition students from the eye-point and voice-point stage to reading in phrases.

Strategy: explicit phrasing

Objectives: Each student will retrain the way his or her eyes look at print. Each student will learn to look at words in groups rather than in isolation. Each student will move from decoding to comprehending.

Directions

Materials
• overhead trans-
  parency/projector
• sheet of paper

1. Use this activity with students who have severe phrasing and fluency problems. Meet with students individually or in small groups for about 3 to 5 minutes daily.

2. In advance, think of a few two-word and three-word phrases (e.g., My school, is red, It has, a big flag). Write them on an overhead transparency.

3. Cover all of the phrases with a sheet of paper, and leave the overhead projector turned off.

4. Tell the student that you will show him or her one phrase for 1 second. (You will need to be fast. Flip the projector on and off so quickly that the student must visually attend to and recognize all words at once. Do not allow time for reading. Make sure your phrases consist of very easy words.)

5. Move the sheet of paper down so only one phrase is showing on the transparency. Flip the projector on and back off QUICKLY, showing only one phrase.

6. Ask the student to say the phrase.

7. Repeat this process with five to eight phrases each day. Increase the number of phrases as the student's learning improves.